TOP ▶ REQUESTED
Family Favorites
SHEET MUSIC

28 SING-ALONG CLASSICS ARRANGED BY DAN COATES

Alfred

Produced by
Alfred Music
P.O. Box 10003
Van Nuys, CA 91410-0003
alfred.com

Printed in USA.

No part of this book shall be reproduced, arranged, adapted, recorded, publicly performed, stored in a retrieval system,
or transmitted by any means without written permission from the publisher. In order to comply with copyright laws, please apply for
such written permission and/or license by contacting the publisher at alfred.com/permissions.

ISBN-10: 1-4706-1699-8
ISBN-13: 978-1-4706-1699-1

Contents by Category

Contents by Title

CHANUKAH

(Chanukah Chag Yafe Kol Kach)

Traditional
Arr. Dan Coates

Joyfully

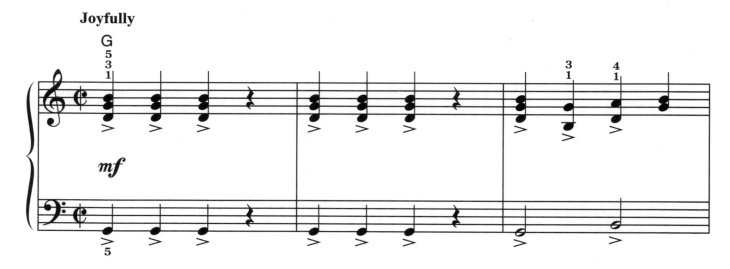

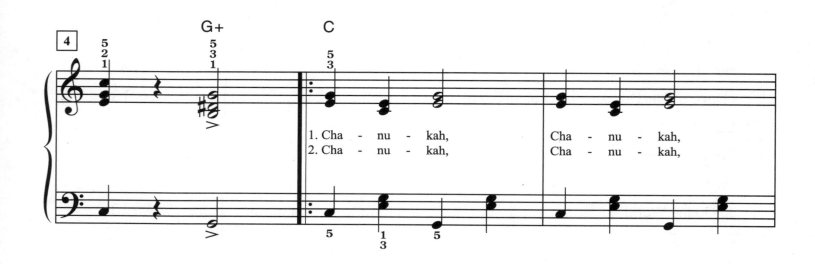

1. Cha - nu - kah,   Cha - nu - kah,
2. Cha - nu - kah,   Cha - nu - kah,

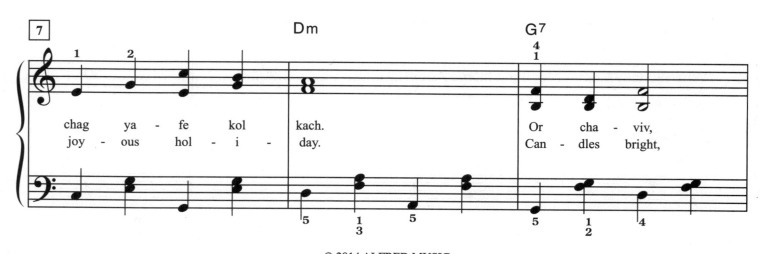

chag   ya - fe kol   kach.   Or   cha - viv,
joy - ous hol - i -   day.   Can - dles bright,

© 2014 ALFRED MUSIC
All Rights Reserved

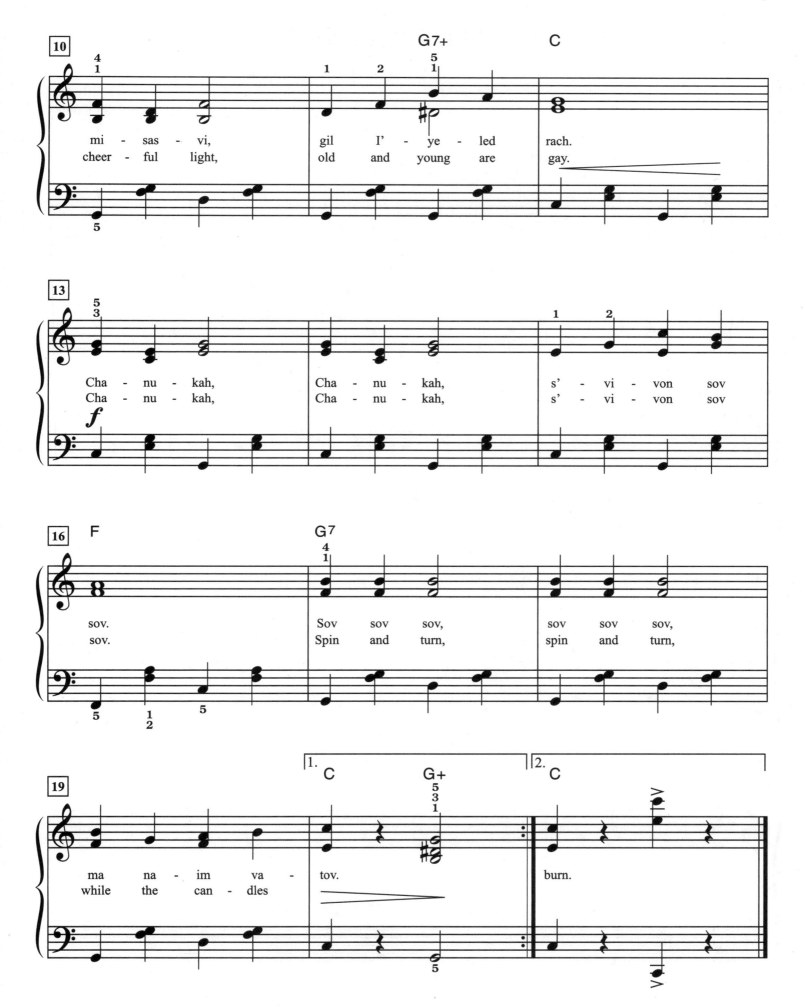

CHANUKAH, OH CHANUKAH

Traditional
Arr. Dan Coates

© 2014 ALFRED MUSIC
All Rights Reserved

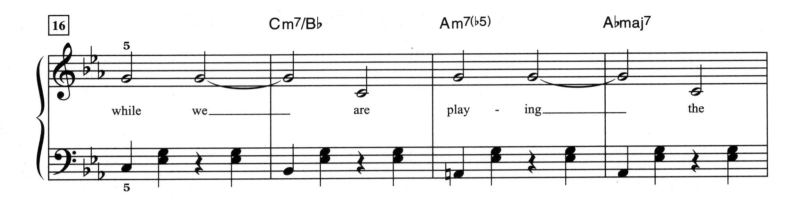

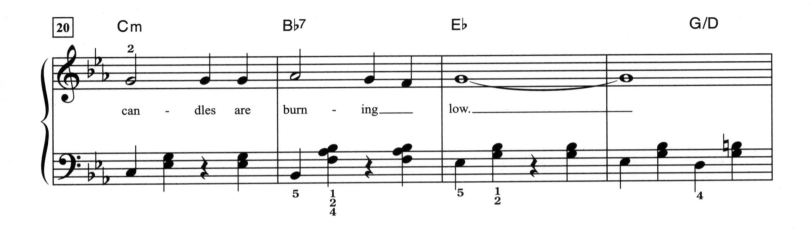

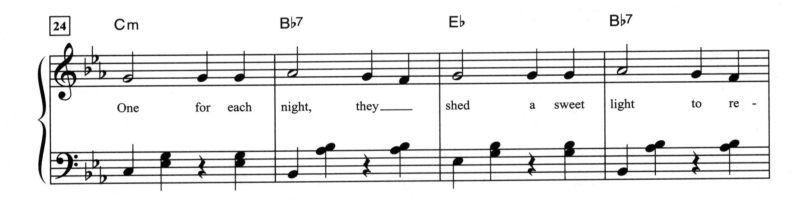

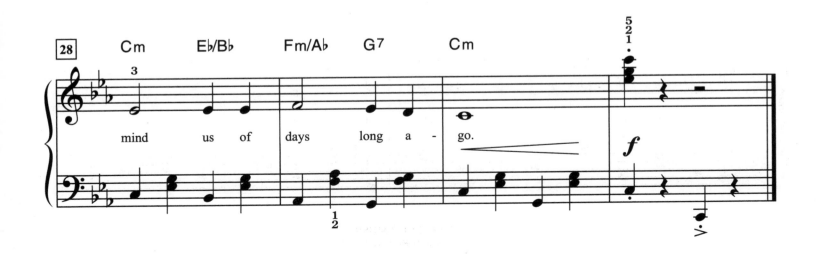

CIELITO LINDO

(My Pretty Darling)

Traditional Mexican Folk Song
Arr. Dan Coates

Moderate waltz

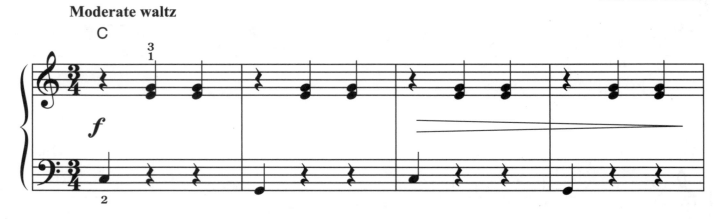

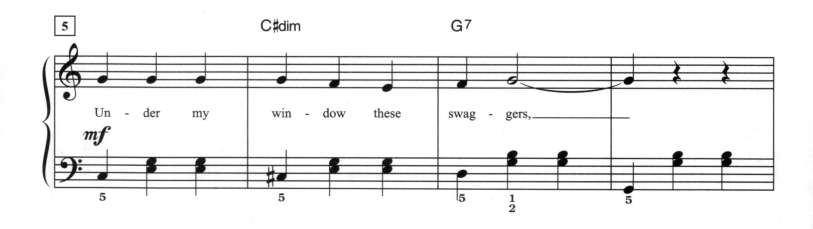

Un - der my win - dow these swag - gers,

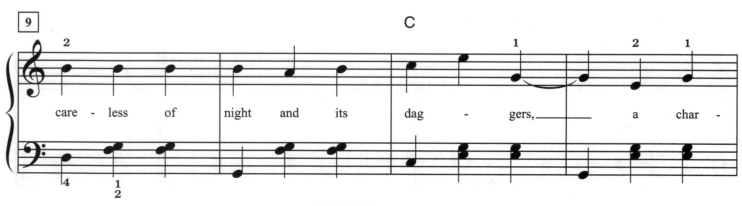

care - less of night and its dag - gers, a char -

© 2014 ALFRED MUSIC
All Rights Reserved

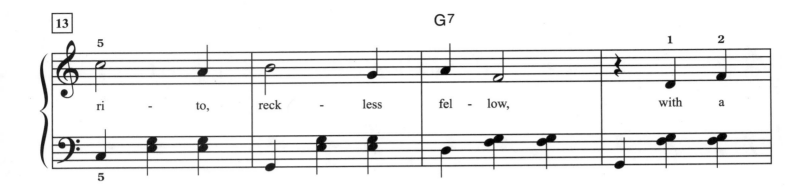

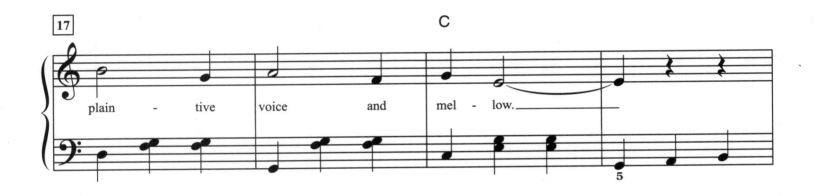

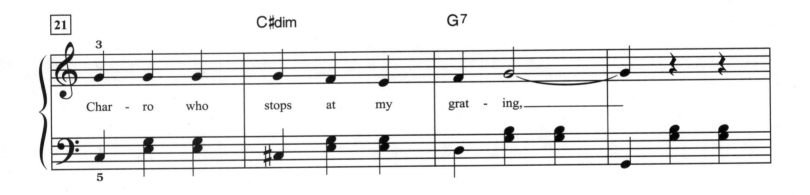

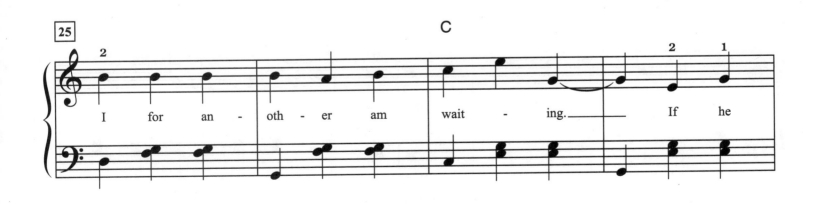

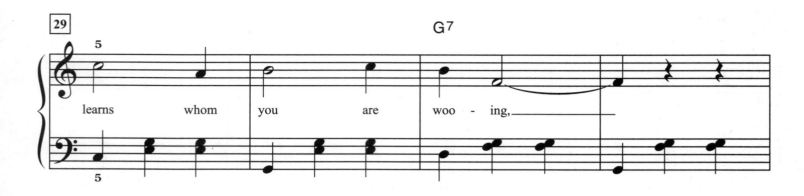

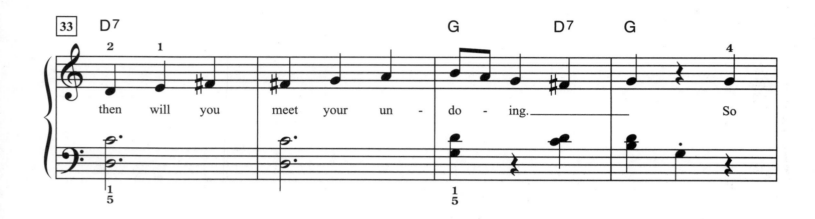

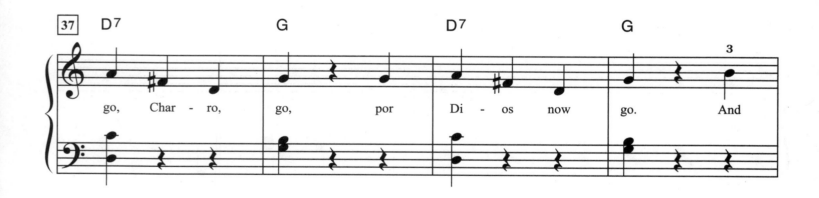

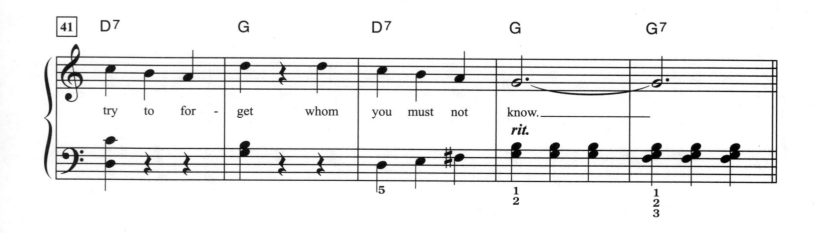

I love a man from fair Coa - hui - la,

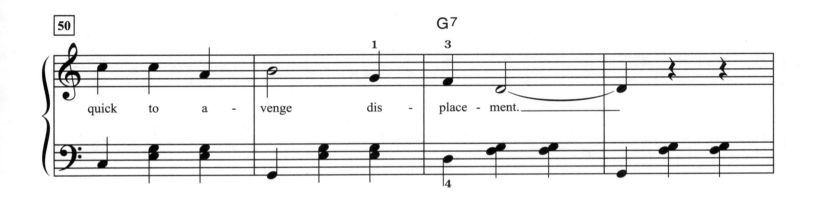

quick to a - venge dis - place - ment.

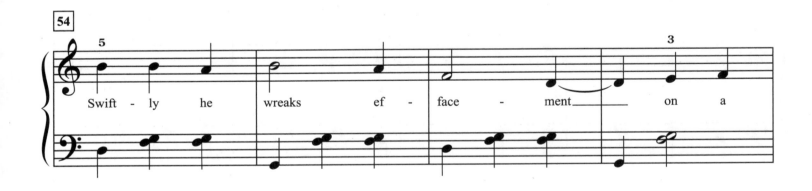

Swift - ly he wreaks ef - face - ment on a

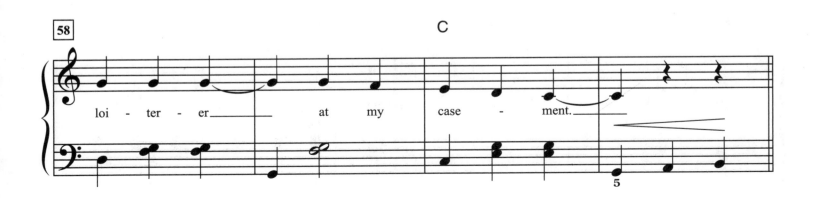

loi - ter - er at my case - ment.

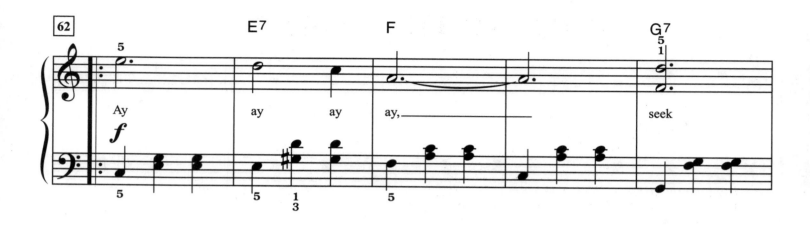

JOY TO THE WORLD

Traditional
Words by ISAAC WATTS
Arr. Dan Coates

© 2014 ALFRED MUSIC
All Rights Reserved

DECK THE HALLS

Traditional
Arr. Dan Coates

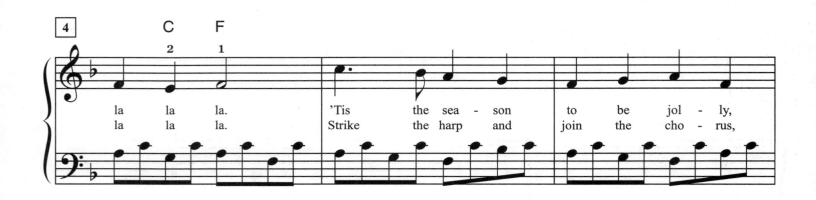

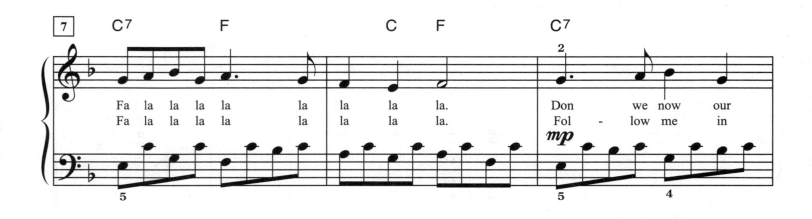

© 2014 ALFRED MUSIC
All Rights Reserved

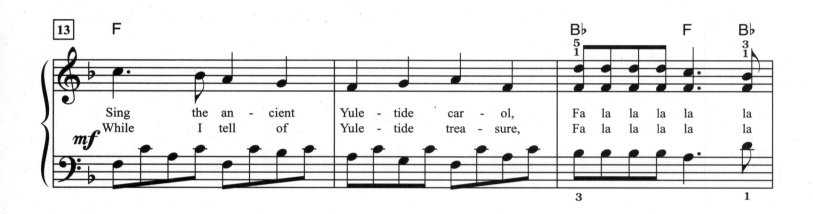

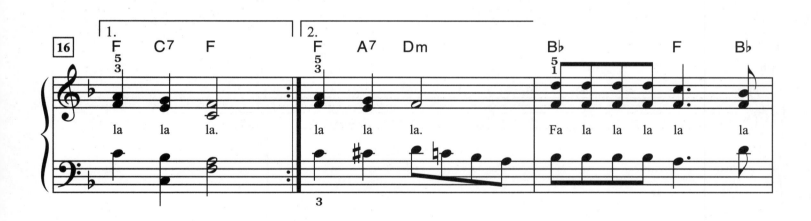

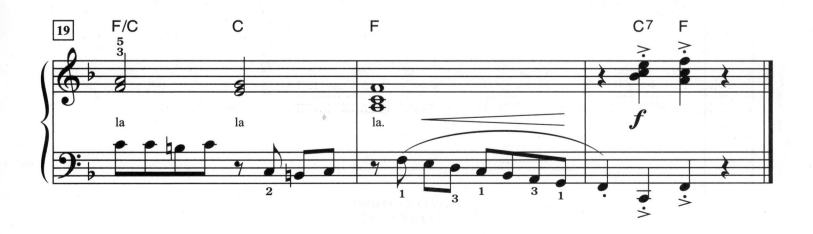

THE FIRST NOEL

Traditional
Arr. Dan Coates

© 2014 ALFRED MUSIC
All Rights Reserved

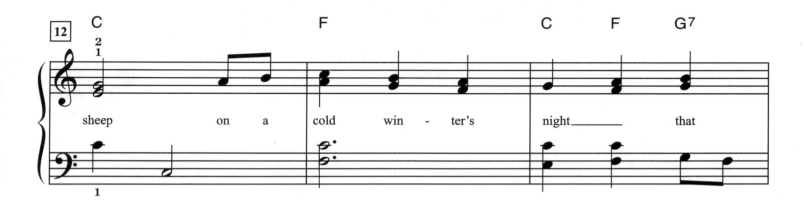

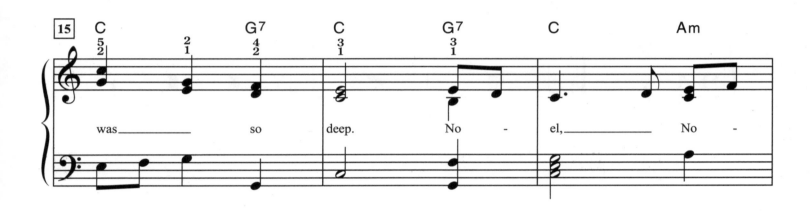

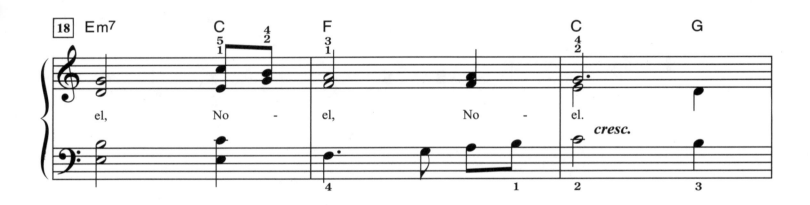

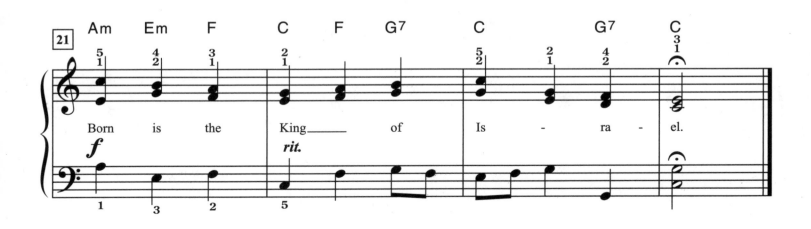

I HAVE A LITTLE DREIDEL

(The Dreidel Song)

Traditional
Arr. Dan Coates

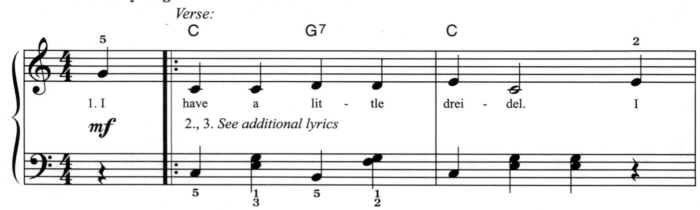

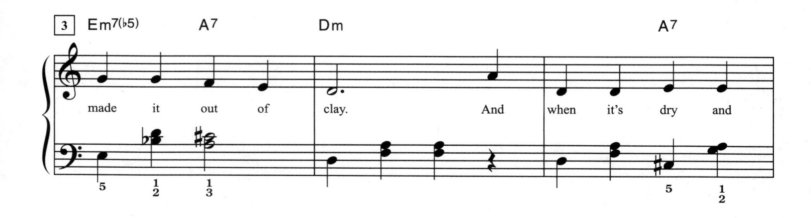

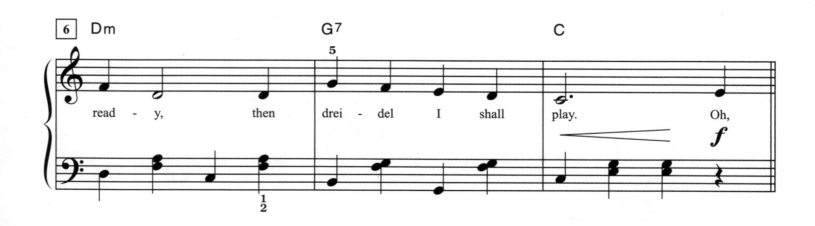

© 2014 ALFRED MUSIC
All Rights Reserved

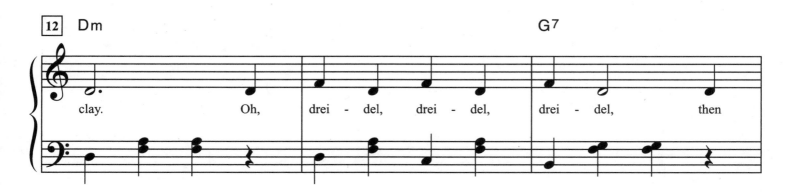

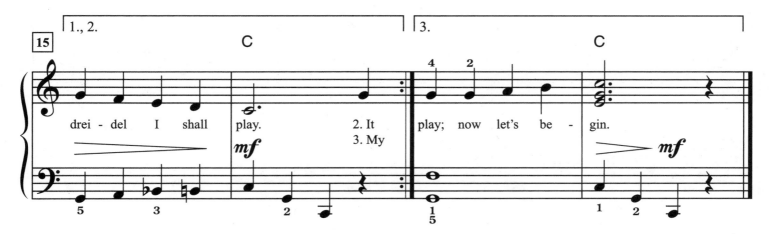

Verse 2:
It has a lovely body,
With legs so short and thin.
And when it gets all tired,
It drops and then I win!

Chorus 2:
Oh, dreidel, dreidel, dreidel,
With legs so short and thin.
Oh, dreidel, dreidel, dreidel,
It drops and then I win!

Verse 3:
My dreidel's always playful;
It loves to dance and spin
A happy game of dreidel.
Come play; now let's begin.

Chorus 3:
Oh, dreidel, dreidel, dreidel,
It loves to dance and spin.
Oh, dreidel, dreidel, dreidel,
Come play; now let's begin.

JINGLE BELLS

Words and Music by JAMES PIERPONT
Arr. Dan Coates

© 2014 ALFRED MUSIC
All Rights Reserved

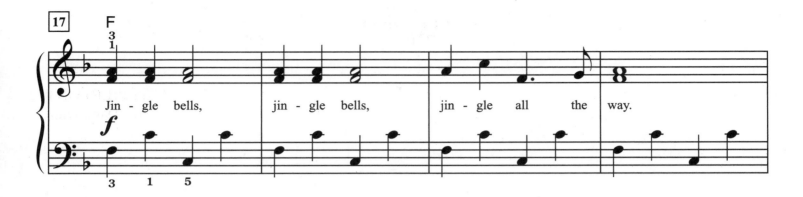

Jin - gle bells, jin - gle bells, jin - gle all the way.

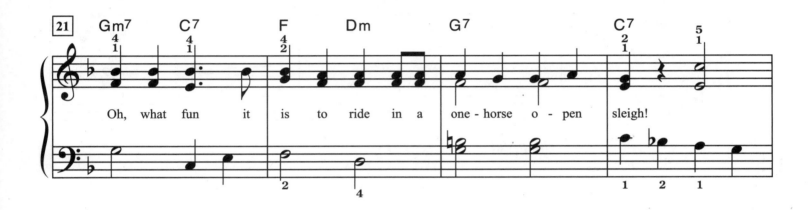

Oh, what fun it is to ride in a one-horse o-pen sleigh!

Jin - gle bells, jin - gle bells, jin - gle all the way.

Oh, what fun it is to ride in a one-horse o-pen sleigh!

THE TWELVE DAYS OF CHRISTMAS

Traditional
Arr. Dan Coates

Brightly

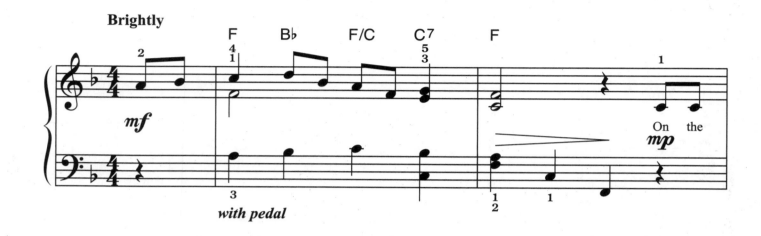

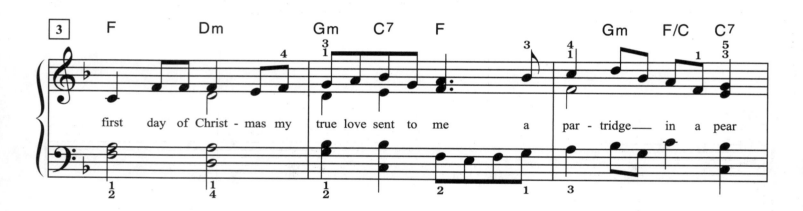

first day of Christ - mas my true love sent to me a par - tridge in a pear

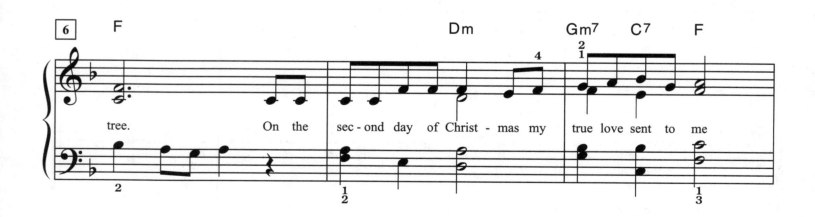

tree. On the sec - ond day of Christ - mas my true love sent to me

© 2014 ALFRED MUSIC
All Rights Reserved

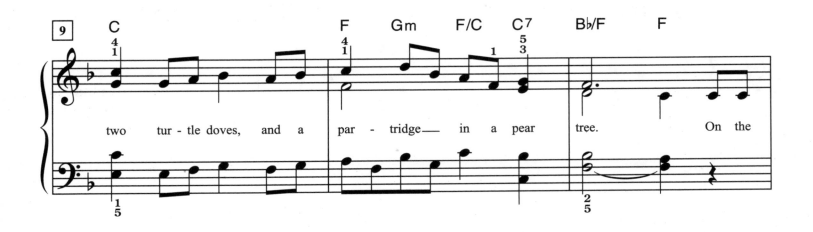

two tur - tle doves, and a par - tridge—— in a pear tree. On the

third day of Christ - mas my true love sent to me three French—— hens,

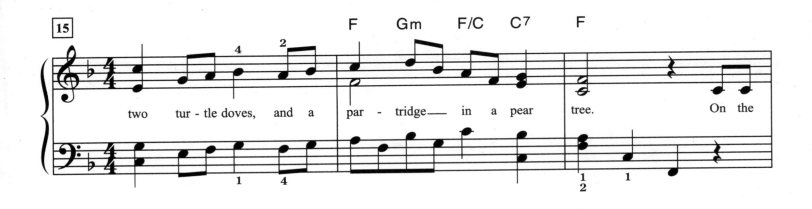

two tur - tle doves, and a par - tridge—— in a pear tree. On the

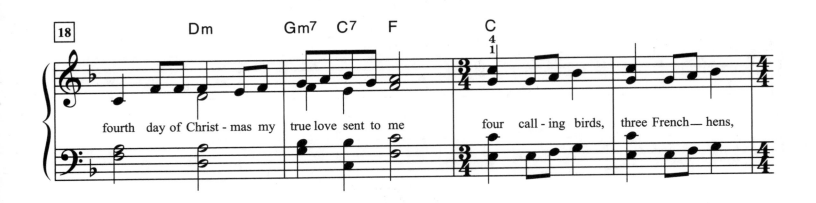

fourth day of Christ - mas my true love sent to me four call - ing birds, three French—— hens,

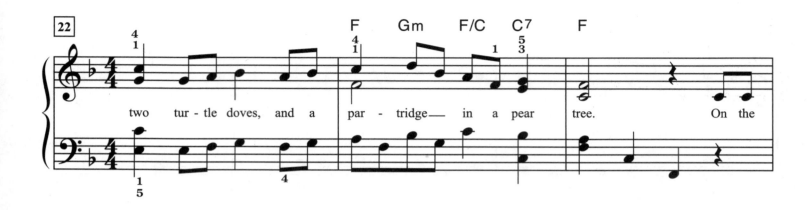

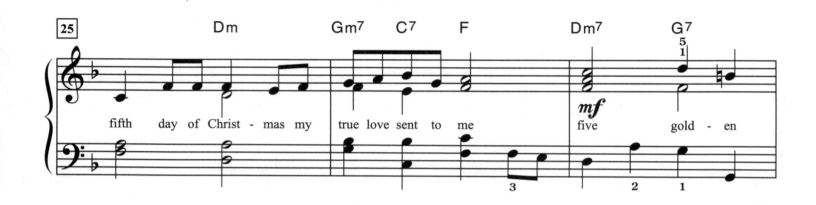

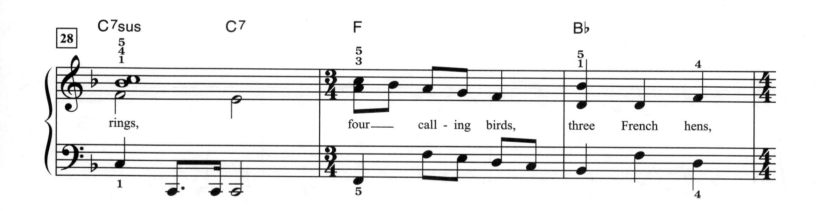

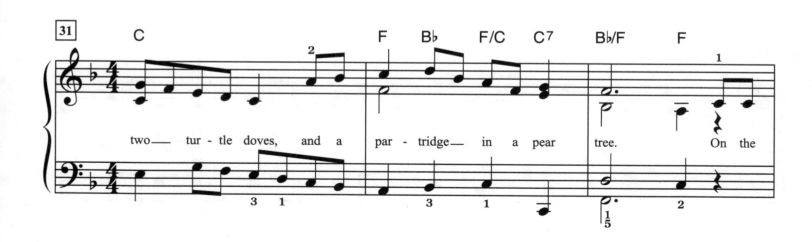

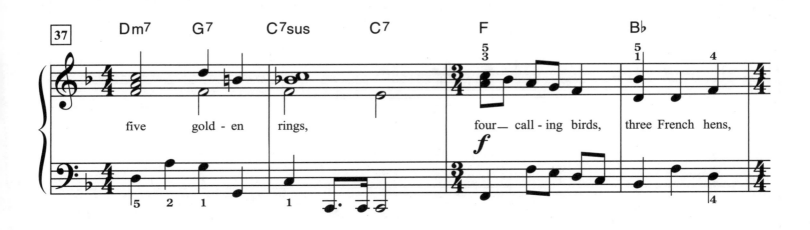

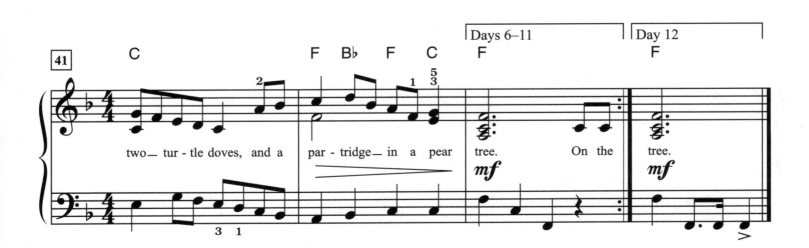

AMERICA THE BEAUTIFUL

Music by KATHERINE LEE BATES
Lyrics by SAMUEL A. WARD
Arr. Dan Coates

© 2014 ALFRED MUSIC
All Rights Reserved

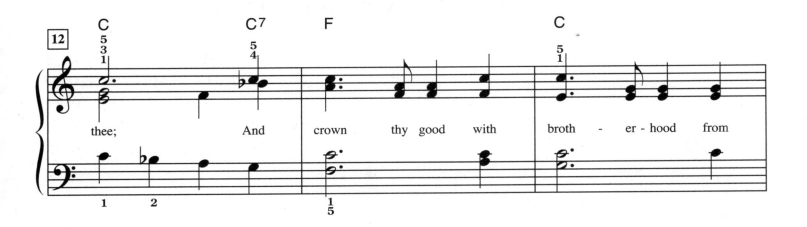

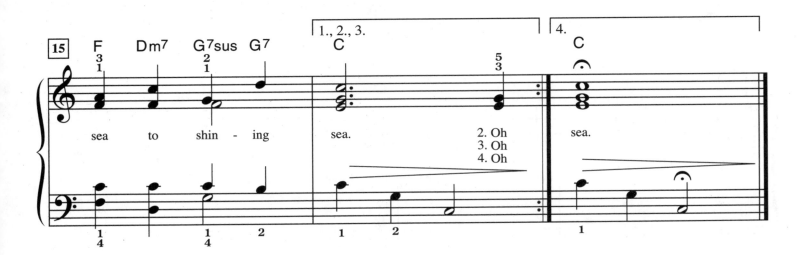

Verse 2:
Oh beautiful for pilgrim feet
Whose stern impassioned stress
A thoroughfare for freedom beat
Across the wilderness.

Chorus:
America! America! God mend thine ev'ry flaw.
Confirm thy soul in self-control,
Thy liberty in law.

Verse 3:
Oh beautiful for heroes proved
In liberating strife.
Who more than self their country loved,
And mercy more than life.

Chorus:
America! America! May God thy gold refine
Till all success be nobleness
And ev'ry gain, divine.

Verse 4:
Oh beautiful for patriot dream
That sees beyond the years.
Thine alabaster cities gleam.
Undimm'd by human tears.

Chorus:
America! America! God shed His grace on thee,
And crown thy good with brotherhood
From sea to shining sea.

THE STAR-SPANGLED BANNER

Words by FRANCIS SCOTT KEY
Music by JOHN STAFFORD SMITH
Arr. Dan Coates

© 2014 ALFRED MUSIC
All Rights Reserved

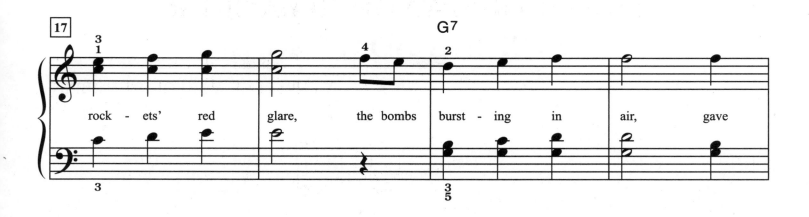

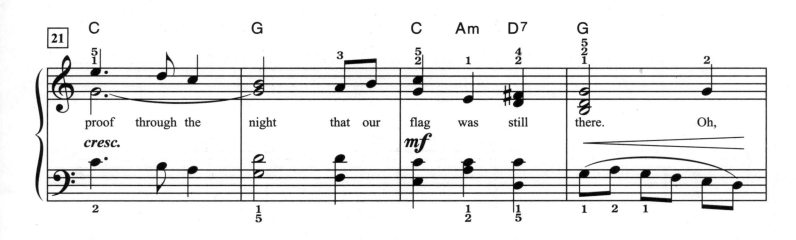

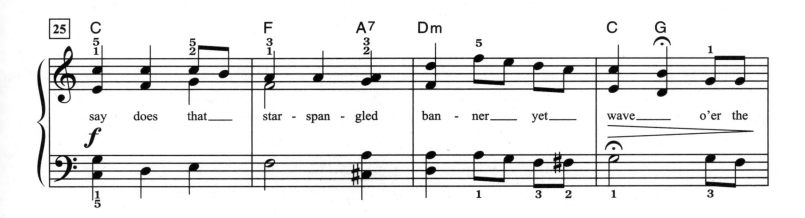

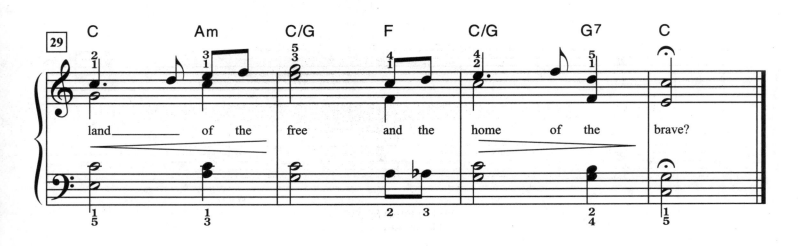

WHEN JOHNNY COMES MARCHING HOME AGAIN

Words and Music by LOUIS LAMBERT
Arr. Dan Coates

© 2014 ALFRED MUSIC
All Rights Reserved

Verse 2:
Oh, Johnny, we say you've been away too long, too long!
We welcome a hero home today with heart and song,
And everyone in the town will cheer,
To show we're happy to have you here.
'Cause we'll feel that way when Johnny comes marching home.

Verse 3:
Get ready to have a jubilee, hurrah! Hurrah!
Get ready with heart so light and free, hurrah! Hurrah!
A laurel wreath we have ready now
To put in place on his loyal brow.
And we'll give three cheers when Johnny comes marching home.

THE YANKEE DOODLE BOY

Words and Music by GEORGE M. COHAN
Arr. Dan Coates

© 2014 ALFRED MUSIC
All Rights Reserved

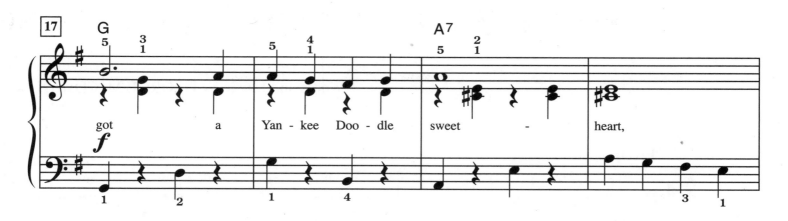

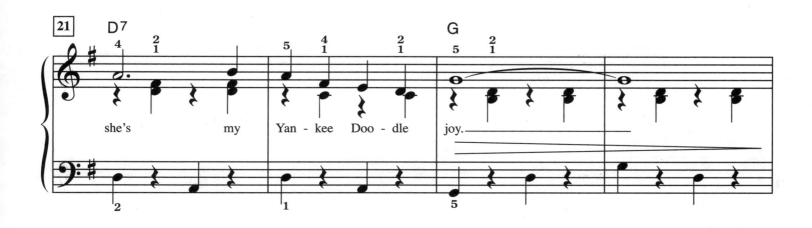

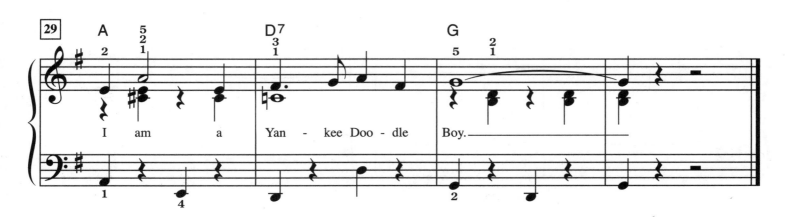

YOU'RE A GRAND OLD FLAG

Words and Music by GEORGE M. COHAN
Arr. Dan Coates

© 2014 ALFRED MUSIC
All Rights Reserved

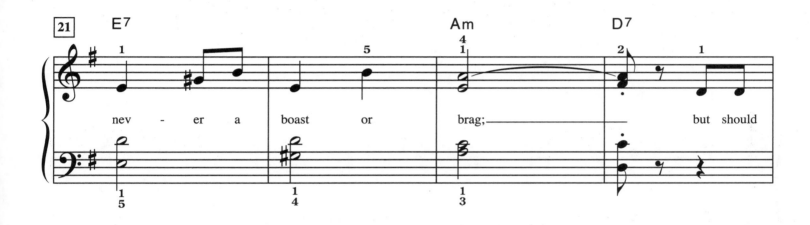

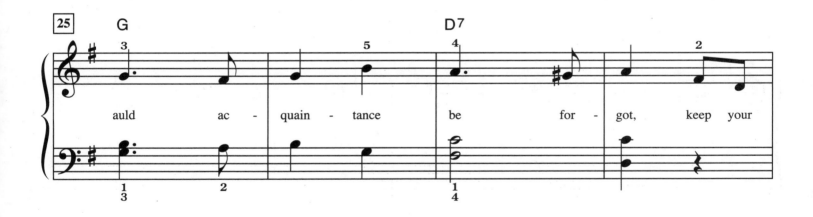

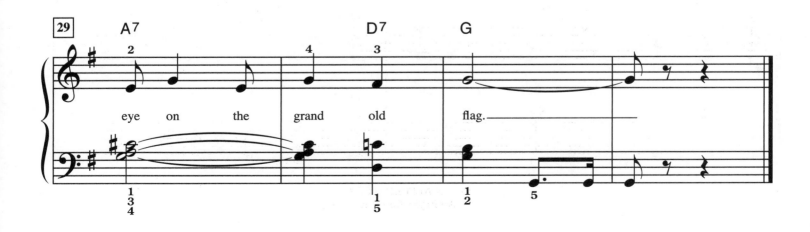

AMERICA
(My Country, 'Tis of Thee)

Traditional Melody
Lyrics by SAMUEL FRANCIS SMITH
Arr. Dan Coates

© 2014 ALFRED MUSIC
All Rights Reserved

AMAZING GRACE

Traditional Hymn
Words by JOHN NEWTON
Arr. Dan Coates

© 2014 ALFRED MUSIC
All Rights Reserved

FOR HE'S A JOLLY GOOD FELLOW

Traditional
Arr. Dan Coates

© 2014 ALFRED MUSIC
All Rights Reserved

DANNY BOY

(Londonderry Air)

Traditional
Arr. Dan Coates

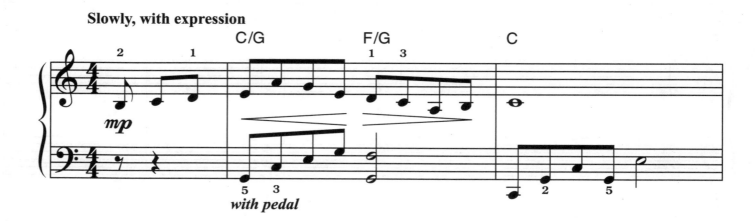

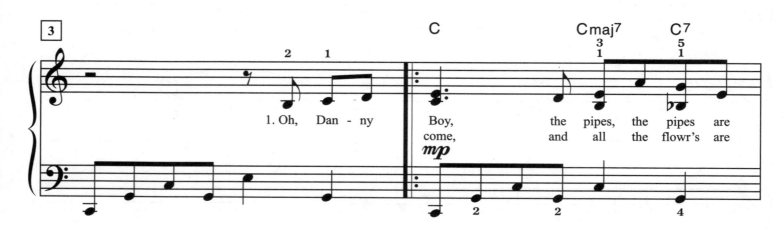

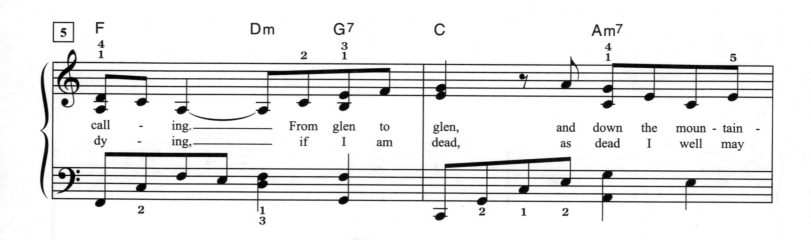

© 2014 ALFRED MUSIC
All Rights Reserved

HAVAH NAGILAH

Traditional
Arr. Dan Coates

© 2014 ALFRED MUSIC
All Rights Reserved

Ha - vah n' - ra - ne - nah. Ha - vah 'n - ra - ne - nah.

Ha - vah 'n - ra - ne - nah, ve - nis - 'me - cha.

Ha - vah 'n - ra - ne - nah. Ha - vah 'n - ra - ne - nah.

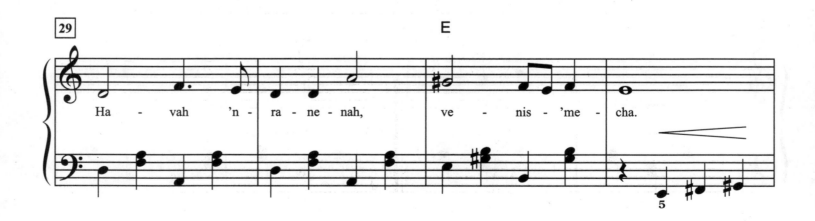

Ha - vah 'n - ra - ne - nah, ve - nis - 'me - cha.

MY WILD IRISH ROSE

Words and Music by CHAUNCEY OLCOTT
Arr. Dan Coates

© 2014 ALFRED MUSIC
All Rights Reserved

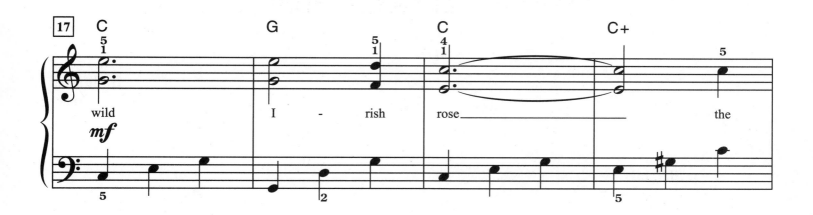

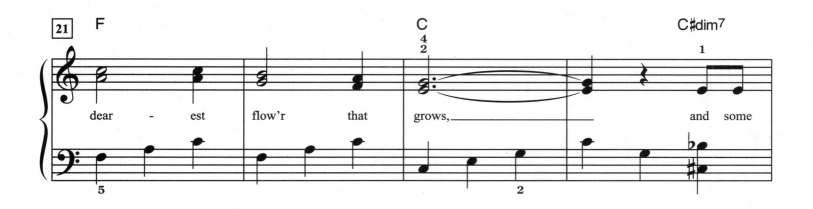

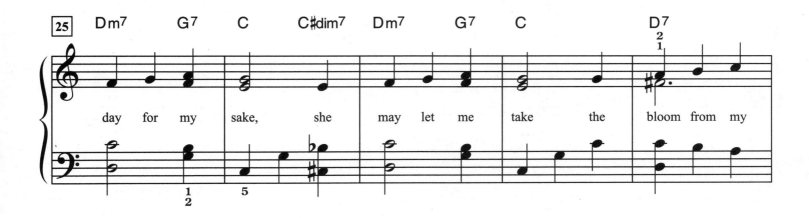

WHEN THE SAINTS GO MARCHING IN

Traditional
Arr. Dan Coates

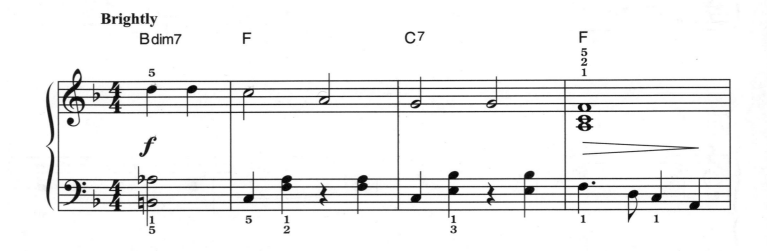

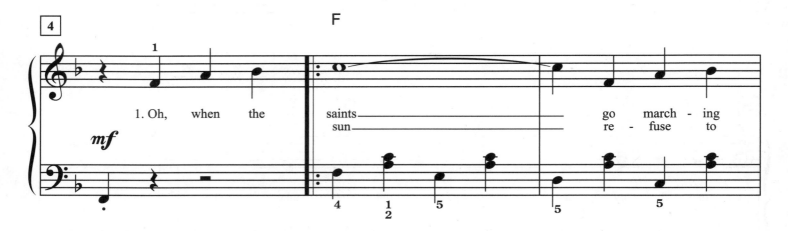

© 2014 ALFRED MUSIC
All Rights Reserved

DO YOUR EARS HANG LOW?

Traditional
Arr. Dan Coates

© 2014 ALFRED MUSIC
All Rights Reserved

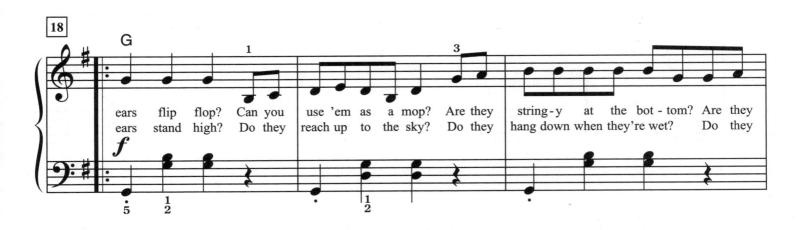

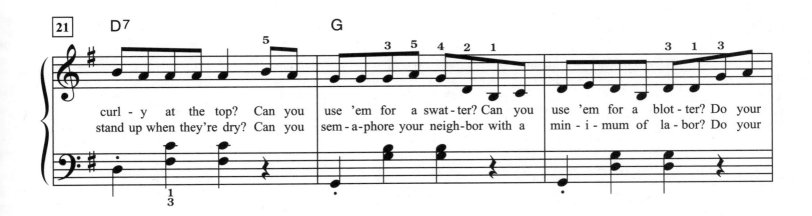

THE FARMER IN THE DELL

Traditional
Arr. Dan Coates

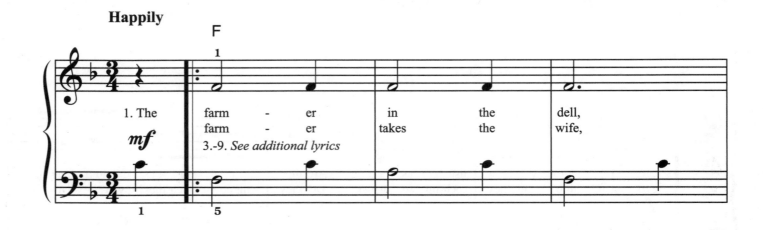

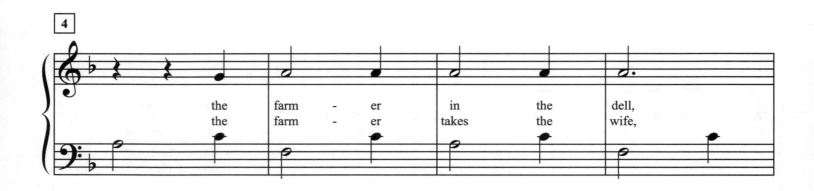

© 2014 ALFRED MUSIC
All Rights Reserved

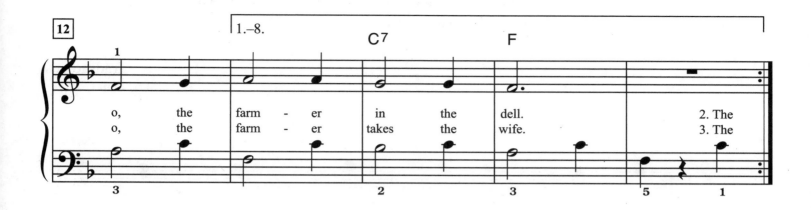

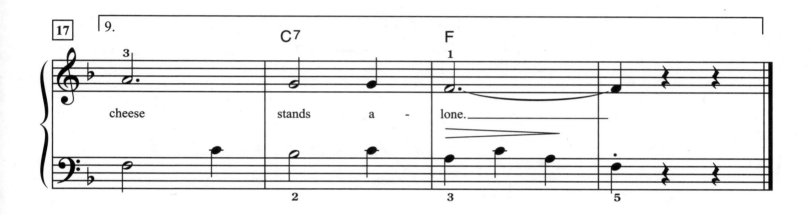

Verse 3:
The wife takes the child,
The wife takes the child,
Hi-ho the dairy-o,
The wife takes the child.

Verse 4:
The child takes the nurse,
The child takes the nurse,
Hi-ho the dairy-o,
The child takes the nurse.

Verse 5:
The nurse takes the dog,
The nurse takes the dog,
Hi-ho the dairy-o,
The nurse takes the dog.

Verse 6:
The dog takes the cat,
The dog takes the cat,
Hi-ho the dairy-o,
The dog takes the cat.

Verse 7:
The cat takes the rat,
The cat takes the rat,
Hi-ho the dairy-o,
The cat takes the rat.

Verse 8:
The rat takes the cheese,
The rat takes the cheese,
Hi-ho the dairy-o,
The rat takes the cheese.

Verse 9:
The cheese stands alone,
The cheese stands alone,
Hi-ho the dairy-o,
The cheese stands alone.

INCY-WINCY SPIDER

Traditional
Arr. Dan Coates

© 2014 ALFRED MUSIC
All Rights Reserved

13 Out came the sun - shine and dried up all the

16 F C7 F rain, and in - cy win - cy spi - der went

19 C7 F up the spout a - gain. *mp*

22 C7 F *sfz* *8va*

I'VE BEEN WORKING ON THE RAILROAD

Traditional
Arr. Dan Coates

© 2014 ALFRED MUSIC
All Rights Reserved

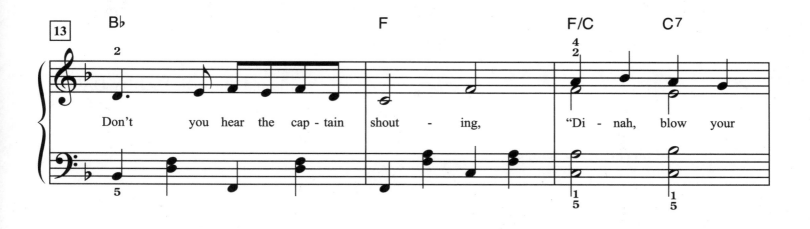

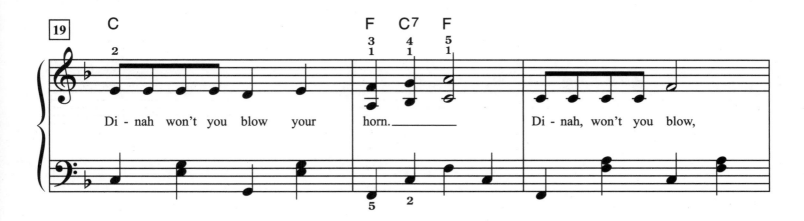

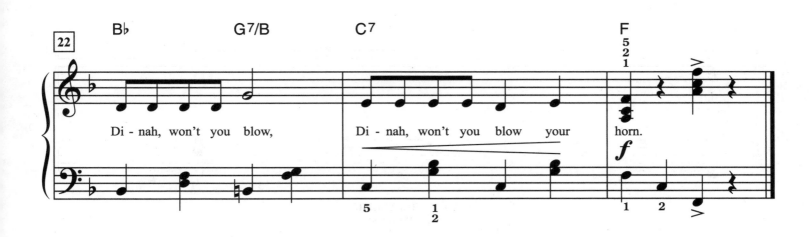

DAISY BELL

(Bicycle Built for Two)

Words and Music by HARRY DACRE
Arr. Dan Coates

Moderate waltz tempo

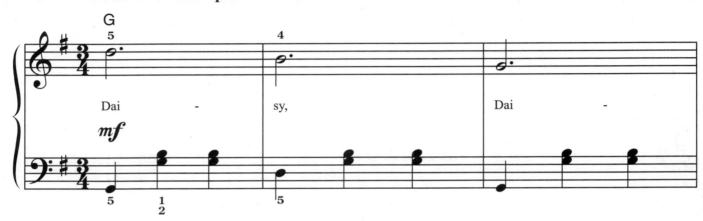

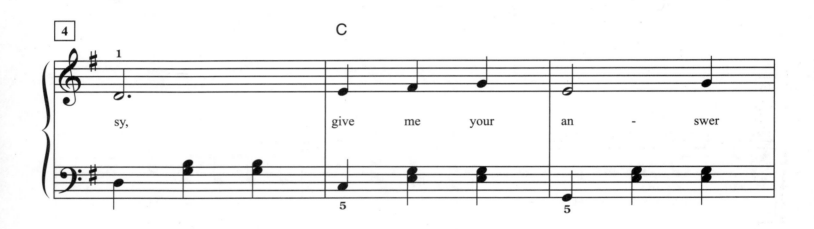

© 2014 ALFRED MUSIC
All Rights Reserved

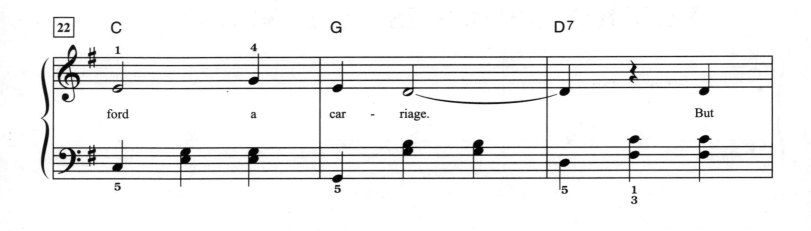

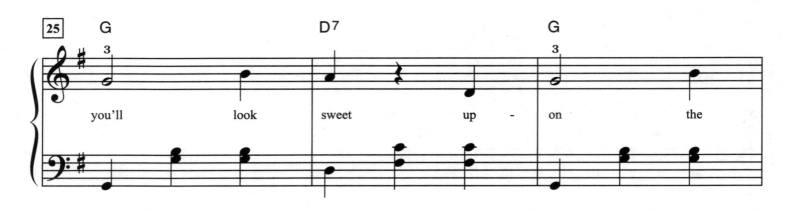

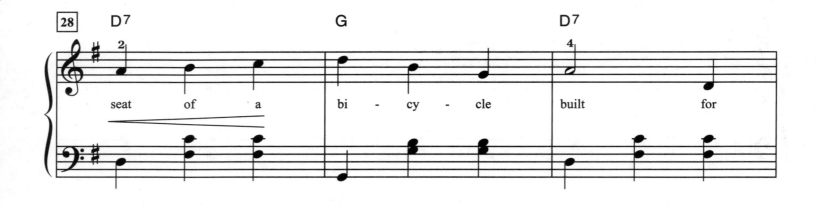

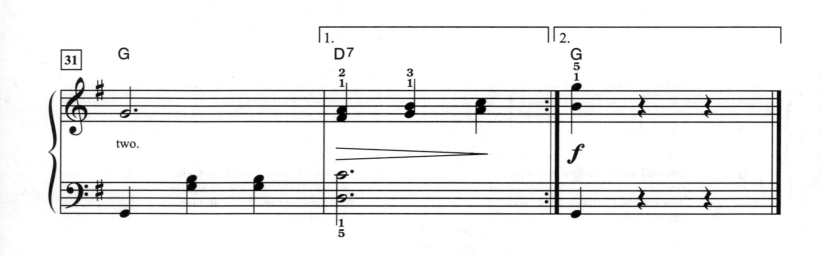

LONDON BRIDGE IS FALLING DOWN

Traditional
Arr. Dan Coates

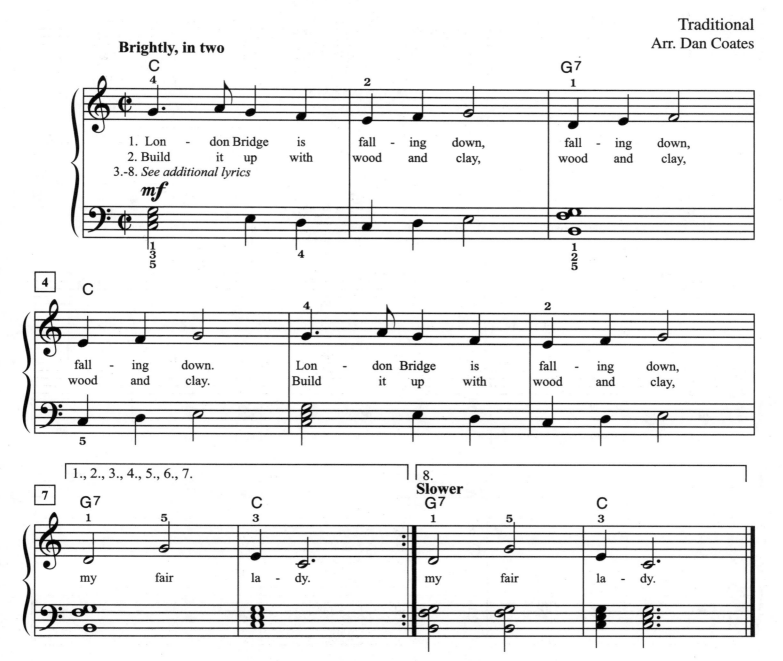

Verse 3:
Wood and clay will wash away,
Wash away, wash away.
Wood and clay will wash away,
My fair lady.

Verse 4:
Build it up with iron and steel,
Iron and steel, iron and steel.
Build it up with iron and steel,
My fair lady.

Verse 5:
Iron and steel will bend and bow,
Bend and bow, bend and bow.
Iron and steel will bend and bow,
My fair lady.

Verse 6:
Build it up with silver and gold,
Silver and gold, silver and gold.
Build it up with silver and gold,
My fair lady.

Verse 7:
Silver and gold will be stolen away,
Stolen away, stolen away.
Silver and gold will be stolen away,
My fair lady.

Verse 8:
Send two men to watch all night,
Watch all night, watch all night.
Send two men to watch all night,
My fair lady.

© 2014 ALFRED MUSIC
All Rights Reserved

TWINKLE, TWINKLE LITTLE STAR

Traditional Melody
Lyrics by JANE TAYLOR
Arr. Dan Coates

© 2014 ALFRED MUSIC
All Rights Reserved

PHOTO CREDITS:
Boy learning how to play the piano: © Shutterstock.com / Andresr
Family playing piano together: © Shutterstock.com / Blend Images
Five happy little kids singing together: © Shutterstock.com / Sergey Novikov
Happy family playing guitar together: © Shutterstock.com / Zurijeta
Happy mother and daughter playing piano together: © Shutterstock.com / arek_malang
Little girl playing guitar with her family at home: © Shutterstock.com / Xavier gallego morell
Man playing piano for his girlfriend: © Shutterstock.com / Minerva Studio
Senior woman together with daughter: © Shutterstock.com / ampyang
Sister teaches brother to play the harmonica: © Shutterstock.com / Fotokostic